A Life Well Loved

Butterfly Rain

BookLeaf Publishing

India | USA | UK

Presentation by *BookLeaf Publishing*

Web: www.bookleafpub.com

E-mail: info@bookleafpub.com

ISBN: 978-93-5744-422-4

First edition 2022

DEDICATION

To those who truly love me, I appreciate you more than you know.

PREFACE

This book started as random thoughts of mine that had a certain melodic feel to them and were stored in the notes app of my phone. When I came across this writing challenge, I knew exactly what to do with them. Enjoy.

Walk Alone

The Earth is filled with wondrous beings
Some don't even know that they are
Somewhere along the way
They were lost
Their energy still resonates
Cold and brash
Haughty and hurried
Still on the brink of death
Their energy drains mine
For I am not strong enough yet
So I walk alone
I look up to share a smile
They look straight ahead
So I follow in kind
But my soul feels the disconnect
It hurts
It feels unnatural
A trillion organisms living on this Earth
Wondrous beings though most know it not
I find one who is like me
One of a few billion
Finally a soul I can relate to
But they don't see anyone they don't know
So I walk alone

Knock Knock

If it's Bliss
Let it in
The Torture of love lost
The Pain of opportunity missed
The Ignorance of time passing
Come and go as they please
So when it comes to visit
In those too few moments
I never hesitate to open my door

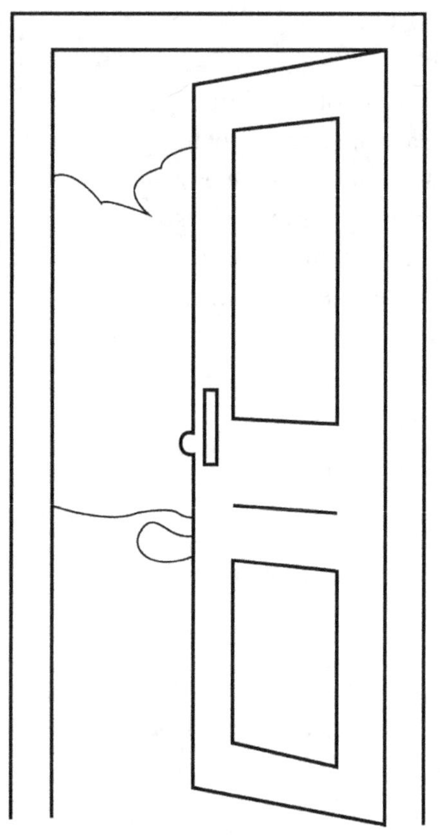

Pride Comes First...

5

I've always been able
To pride myself
On being able to walk away
But surprisingly for once
I've met someone
Who's begging me to stay

Shadows

I prefer the openness
Corners are too confining
Sharp edges keep you firm in place
No light keeps you from shining

But once that bind was comfy
You know who you are
You know where you belong
With the shadows by far

I don't remember the day
Nor the exact hour
Don't remember if I wept
When I decided to take back my power

Secrets were no longer attractive
Shadows held me down
Freedom feels best
I know for sure now

Wind Blows, Hair Grows

It's been a long time
I acknowledge this fact
It is great to see you
I can tell you that
Things have been fine
No fluff no distress
I hope it's the same for you
All laughs no regrets
Do I still work where?
Why yes I do
Do you still live
On that same street too?
Funny how time flies
And some things stay the same
We live and we learn
We love some new names
Yes my hair has grown
It's funny you should mention
Yours has grown too
Yes I paid attention
Your hair always grows?

I'd say that's a coincidence
Mine always does too
With no alter incidents
Wind blows, hair grows
That's just life
It happens to everyone
Black, yellow, red or white
Oh I see what you mean
You think since I'm this tone
My hair doesn't grow
It doesn't get this long
Well I'm proud to show you
How silly that sounds
You only know my name and race
You know nothing of my background
But it has been great to see you
I hope we cross paths again
I'm sorry though I must be going
I'm supposed to be meeting a true friend

Coward

I don't like loving you
It's selfish to admit
Every time you leave my side
My heart breaks just a bit

A Living Death

I can't live an unhappy life
You know those moments
Where you grin and bear it?
I've never had one

Each moment of sadness
Is its own death to me
My spirit dies and withers
Until I can emerge again

Bailey

The purest moments?
When I yawn and stretch
Only to glance over at you
Doing the same
Then you sit upright
Looking deep into my eyes
Waiting for a signal
Forever with the shits
The world will never know
Our deep wordless conversations
Between two spirits who found each other
Different species though we may be
If I shake my head no
You'll lay back down
If I get out the bed
You bound out of yours
And we're off to a new day
With the best new adventures in store

Rose Colored Shades

Your love for me keeps me going
In my random look off moments
I think of you and smile

No day is too gloomy
I'm never too moody
Feeling all looney
Your love transcends all

What did I do?
Some time when I wasn't paying attention
Some where I helped a stranger and didn't
realize
Some how I pleased Cupid
What did I do to deserve you?

I know you're not perfect
But for me you are
Through all hard times you're worth it
My North Star

Hopelessly
Unequivocally
Maniacally even
I am in love with you

Each Day

In the still of the night
I wake and I thrive
I come alive
In the still of the night

In the morning's light
I bask and stretch
The world's not a mess
In the morning's light

At the height of the sun
I fly and I run
But soon I'll be done
At the height of the sun

At the time of dusk
I moan and I fuss
There's too little time
At the time of the dusk

In the still of the night
I get sleep that I fight
Hope another day will arrive
In the still of the night

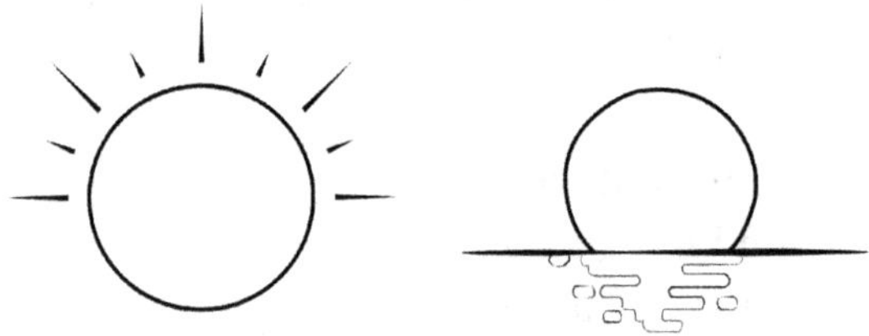

Action

Plotting on a feeling
Thinking of an action
Watching you sleep
I ponder your reaction

Moving so slowly
Crawling on all fours
Racing my beating heart
To where your love will overflow

Pulling it all down
Raising you up
Motioning back and forth
Soon you'll wake up

The Big Screen

I hate watching movies
I get lost in a world that has to end
And my only choices left are
Come back to my boring world
Or get lost in another
That won't ever quite measure up

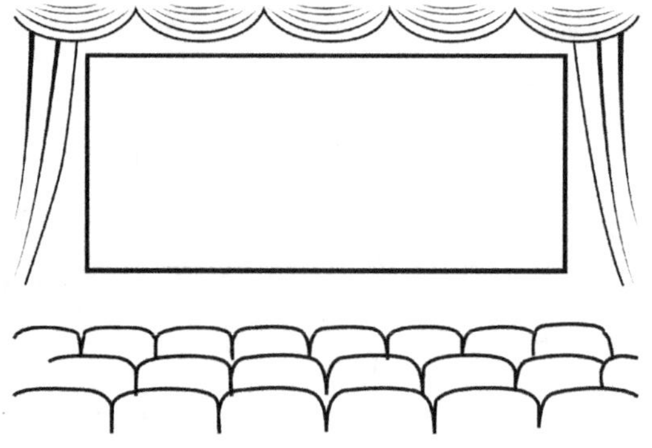

The Crown

My hair is the color of my soul
Its length is the stretch of my energy
Its texture my heart's intricacies

Stuck

We go no deeper
We drift no higher
Something's holding us back
From innermost desires

The love is there
The angst is too
But every time we're together
I'm no deeper into you

Floating on the surface
Just seems to work best
Let any disagreements go
Just give it a rest

I can't give my all
When it's never matched
I can't let go either
Dammit I'm attached

Nowhere to go
No idea what to do
And you have no solutions
You're just stuck to me too

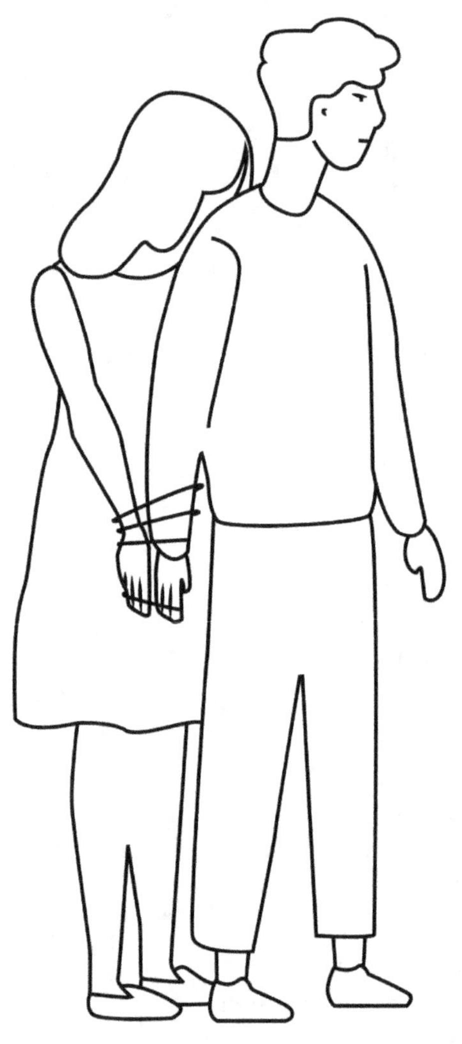

Aspiration

Sign your name here
Please leave your identity at the door
You won't be yourself anymore
So many other choices are in store

Have a seat, dear
Here's a new face to try on
All of your past is long gone
The clothes? Oh, a standard add-on

Let's get your body in gear
Don't make that look with your face
Every single hair has its place
There's no room for mistakes

Pose and smile, you hear?
Prettier friends are now with you
Vacation with your new love too
All of your dreams have come true

Society is waiting

Right through those double doors
Your life is no longer yours
Cameras watch your every step

Fans only love you for your rep

Scrutiny on your breakfast plate
Then all the love turns into hate
The money leaves and so do they
No longer careful with what they say

Mentally deteriorating

Withdrawal

I've never experienced it
But I'm going to bet
Drug withdrawals are easier
Than emotional ones
At least with drugs
You know how long you'll be miserable

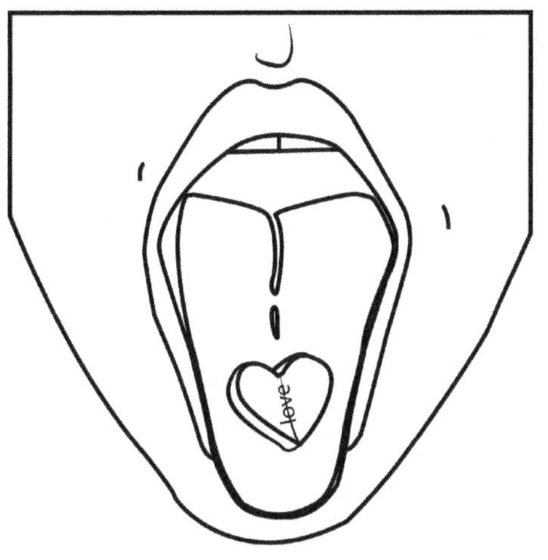

love

Ten Percent

When you come to find out
That what you think matters
Is only ten percent
Perspectives change

The remaining ninety
Is actually on you
And how you decide to move
Choose wisely

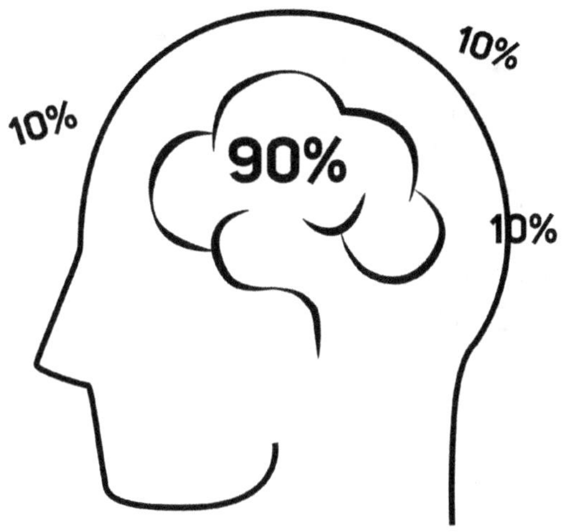

10%
10%
90%
10%

Façade

Just a boy
Trying to be a man
Trying to love me
Difficultly

Just a girl
Trying to be a woman
Trying to know love
Wholly

Just some anger
Trying to hide fear
Trying to hide grief
Terribly

But, I love you!
I love you!

False Remedy

I took a pill yesterday
It did not cure my woes
It did not kill my foes
It didn't tickle my toes

I had a drink last night
Family was no dearer
Brain was no clearer
Vision was a bit nearer

Today I gave myself a prick
I fainted right away
I woke up the next day
Everyone asked was I okay
The hospital made me stay

I had no idea I was that sick.

Friendly Reminder

I hope I remind you to breathe
When you look at me
Moments before you were holding your breath
Tension brought on by the chaos of the world
That you hadn't planned on

I hope I remind you to think
Elbows are what everyone puts forward first
Not necessarily their best foot as long thought
I am a spiritual being like you in clay form
Courtesy is never old-fashioned

I hope I remind you to listen
White noise comes often
You must protect yourself from the nonsense
I get it I do
But worthwhile messages drift in too

I hope I remind you to live
After a long day of work is over
After the headache has come and gone
Pull out your pen or headphones or paintbrush
And remind yourself that you're alive

And more

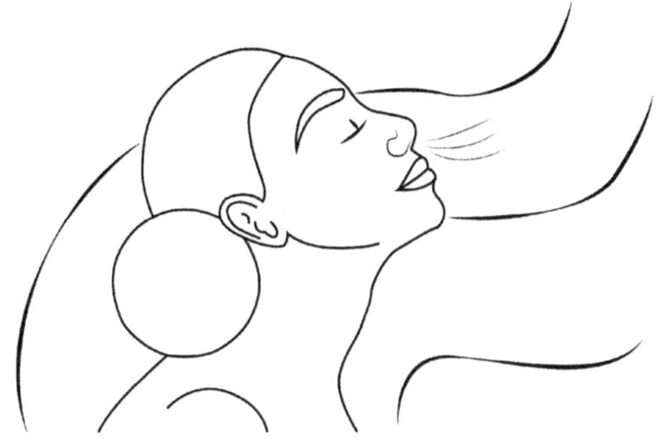

Namesake

Funny how the breeze
Only has to come through once
And nothing is ever the same
Again.